To Shirley

Hope you
enjoy my
Book
With
Love

Marilyn

PATCHWORK PIECES, VOL. II,
(More threads of my Life)

PATCHWORK PIECES, VOL. II,
(More threads of my Life)

By

Marilyn Lowden Koss Wright - 2013

Marilyn Lowden Koss Wright

ISBN 978-1-300-59064-4

This book is dedicated to:

The Elmgrove Girls.... Carol Mitchell Logan
Joan Vanderbeck Maier
Velma Bridgeman Thiele
(In loving Memory)

Four little girls who journeyed life together,
Friends Forever...
Infinity and Beyond!

And to

My Special Friend

You are the one who encouraged me....
You are the one who helped me work
Thru my doubts....
You are the one I could count on....
You are Special....
You know who you are...
And I thank you.

FORWARD

In 2009 my first book, "Patchwork Pieces" was published. While waiting for copies to arrive, I wrestled with emotions not unlike waiting the birth of a child. I was excited, yet apprehensive and could not wait for the day to arrive. The anticipation ended on a pretty fall day when the Fed Ex truck delivered four large boxes.

My granddaughter, Paige, was with me when the Fed Ex truck arrived. I was delighted she was able to share my lifelong dream as it became a reality. However, the emotion for which I was not prepared was my own reaction to my dream as I gingerly took the first copy from the carton.

Unlike the birth of your child where you just want to keep looking at your creation I was suddenly struck with an over whelming desire to hide the boxes in a closet before anyone else saw them. While my feelings were unexplainable, my confidence was gone. After all, I reasoned, who would want to read about me?

Just about this time a friend arrived. Bursting through the door, my friend immediately spied the book and began to congratulate me. I promptly interrupted blurting out my fears. What if I did not possess the talent I thought I had? What if no one liked anything about my book? Perhaps I had shared too many intimate details of my life. My friend continued to try to be encouraging but I just could not be reassured.

The uneasiness continued through a sleepless night when suddenly I had an idea. I should find someone whom I trusted completely, someone I knew would tell me the truth. I knew just the person, my brother, Roger. I was confident that both he and my sister-in-law, Marilyn would be, perhaps painfully, honest. Yes, my sister-in-law's name is Marilyn. Our family seems to be like Daryl, Daryl and Daryl as we have several same names not to mention birthdays which are repeated.

The following morning, I dashed to their house with copies of Patchwork Pieces. I then anxiously waited to hear their thoughts. To my delight both separately gave the book a thumbs-up. My confidence returned and I felt I was ready for family, friends and the general public.

The experience has not only been gratifying but extremely humbling. I have received comments, telephone calls, notes and emails which have been amazing. It is especially exciting when someone mentions they were reminded of a special time in their lives or perhaps I jogged a long forgotten memory. Thank you all.

Since the publication of the book I have joined an internet group called Writer's on the Loose where I write a blog called Musings by Marilyn. As I continued to write I realized there were more stories to share so decided to embark on this endeavor.

It is my hope that you will enjoy Patchwork Pieces Volume II, More threads of my Life.

Sincerely, Marilyn Lowden Koss Wright

INDEX

THOSE HAZY, LAZY, CRAZY DAYS OF SUMMER

Growing up in the fifties was the best. Summers at our cottage on Alder Beach were outstanding. Once settled at the cottage, our shoes were kicked off; a bathing suit became the daily attire and laughter the fare. We kids were free to wander the shores of Lake Ontario as long as we re-appeared at noon and five. No cell phones, in fact no telephone at all. I won't even mention indoor plumbing, because you guessed it, there was none.

For ten wonderful weeks, we were free. Free to search for sea glass, swim with our friends, go boating or walk the shoreline in search of something. Sometimes we found nothing more than an unusual piece of driftwood. Roger and I were really fortunate since the Bridgeman and Mitchell families from our Elmgrove neighborhood had cottages within walking distance.

Although we were free to wander as we pleased, our parents did set perimeters. We could go west to Hilton Beach or east to Lighthouse Beach. Girls were to travel in pairs and check in with someone's mother every couple hours and there was no swimming without supervision. One of my favorite walks was to the lighthouse on Lighthouse Beach.

Originally named the Bogus Point Light, the magnificent lighthouse towered majestically in the sky. At the time the light was a working light. I felt comforted when I woke in the middle of the night and could see the rotating light searching the waters. Since my father had told many stories about the rum-runners during prohibition; my imagination went wild when I saw some little boat far out on the lake. I spent countless nights dreaming up romantic stories about some vessel that only existed in my mind.

One day while walking to Lighthouse Beach I was delighted to meet Flora Millar. Flora lived in my beloved lighthouse.

Her father was a civilian Coast Guard employee who managed lighthouses on the Great Lakes. She invited us to the lighthouse where we climbed to the very top. Convinced I could see the other side of the lake, I fell in love that day, a love that has continued all of my life. Not only have I collected lighthouses but have been able to visit several and found something unique about each.

Flora married her childhood sweetheart, Al Bishop, and together raised their family right here in Hilton, NY on Moul Road. We have remained friends and as the circle of life evolves her sons are now close friends with my son, Roger.

Today the lighthouse is a delightful bed & breakfast, the original tower gone, although one of the owners did rebuild a portion of it. The house is absolutely charming as it is decorated to recapture the flavor of days gone by. As for me, the old Bogus Point Light will continue to shine forever in my mind.

Another favorite haunt of ours was the merry-go-round located at Wautoma Beach. Alvie Miller and his wife owned and operated the merry-go-round in addition to a little corner store. Well, actually Mr. Miller operated the merry-go-round while the first Mrs. Miller, a large woman with a stern disposition, ran the store. You automatically knew you should say please and thank you. My friends and I spent as little time as possible in the store and actually that was fine as we were were far more interested in riding the merry-go-round.

Mr. Miller (we called him Alvie) seemed to cringe a little when he saw our group arriving to jump on his ride with hopes of catching the brass ring. That treasure assured you of a couple free rides. In all fairness to Alvie, I would have cringed too. While not being nasty our gang, especially the boys, kidded him unmercifully. For the most part Alvie took the kidding well although once in a while one of the boys would get mouthy and find himself kicked off the ride.

I am not sure when the merry-go-round closed; although I think it was the early sixties. Many years ago, while visiting a friend who lived close to the boarded up ride, we walked over to peek through the cracks of the boards only to see broken benches, dirt, dust and spiders. The colorful carousel animals were gone and just a few of the posts remained.

The sadness I felt as I peered through the cracks was quickly replaced by a memory I suddenly re-lived. The merry, merry music of the merry-go-round was blaring and the ride was full of happy, laughing kids. Alvie was collecting tickets when suddenly someone yelled, "I got the brass ring!"

The ride came to a slow stop as Alvie retrieved the coveted ring and announced the next ride was the last for the night. Aren't memories great?

After the first Mrs. Miller died Alvie moved into the Village of Hilton where he met and married a woman who had been a live-in babysitter for my friend, Minerva (Mickey) O'Connor. Not only was Betty Mickey's babysitter but they became close friends so much so that Betty became part of Mickey's family. Alvie passed first so when Betty passed years later my friend Mickey found herself the executrix of the estate. Going through personal belongings Mickey came across a brass ring and a rubber stamp from the old merry-go-round. Mickey, not originally from the area, knew I had spent many happy hours at the merry-go-round so asked if I would like them. I was so pleased I purchased a small replica of a carousel horse to which I have attached the brass ring and I display it with the merry-go-round stamp.

Seldom were we bored during those hazy, lazy, crazy days of summer as there always seemed to be something to do. When we were not in the lake or boating we played cards. After the sun created a magnificent sunset we would build a bonfire. Everyone, adults and kids, would sit around the fire until the soft lapping of the water lulled us to sleep. Starlit nights inspired discussions of the planets and constellations. On rare occasions the northern lights would dance in the sky almost as though they had been sent to entertain Alder Beach that particular night.

On a stormy or rainy night we often went to the movies as there was a movie theater in Village of Hilton. Once the movie ended everyone congregated at the Candy Kitchen on Main Street to enjoy a soda or hot fudge sundaes until our ride arrived. I suspect if the walls at the old Candy Kitchen could talk we would hear some great stories as it was obviously the place to be. I will bet some life-long romances might have had their beginning at the Candy Kitchen.

The Village of Hilton was a sleepy, quiet town back then and Main Street thrived. There were grocery stores, the Pleasure Shop, a general store, the post office, bank, Brinkel's drugstore and Stothard's hardware. The huge fire in 1965 changed a large part of the Village as well as small business owners became unable to compete with chain stores so the Village of today looks very different than it did.

My thoughts of summers long ago would not be complete if I did not write my memories of Manitou Beach. Manitou Beach is located at the end of Manitou Beach Road which is in the town of Greece, NY. My involvement with Manitou Beach began at age fourteen when I worked for Edna Weidman at her ice cream stand. At that time Edna and her brother George owned the Elmheart Hotel, a property which had been in their family since the early 1900's.

During the early years of the century and continuing through some of the forties, Manitou Beach was one of the ultimate playgrounds for summer fun. The beach which was the last stop on the trolley line that originated at Charlotte and ended at Manitou Beach swarmed with visitors especially on the weekends. There were two hotels, the Odenbach and the Elmheart both noted for fine dining and great accommodations. In addition there was a private club, the Colony Club. Also there was a large water slide, rides, the ice cream stand, and an outdoor dance pavilion. At the south end of the beach there was a camping area. Recently I was told that out on the peninsula there were several summer cottages which eventually were moved to the shores of Braddock's Bay. Manitou Beach, without a doubt buzzed with excitement from May until Labor Day.

If one were to travel by car or buggy to the beach they traveled east toward the lake on Manitou Beach Road. When one was approximately a quarter of mile from the lake they drove through a row of huge poplar trees which adorned both sides of the road. The wonderful trees, which rustled in the breezes, created the ambience of traveling through an elegant, graceful entrance to something spectacular and you were. The outdoor dance pavilion was located on the south side of the road behind the poplar trees. In the late twenties, many famous big bands of the era played at the dance pavilion including Benny Goodman and Glenn Miller.

While the poplars still existed all of the rest of the elegance and excitement was a thing of the past during my youth. The Odenbach Hotel was completely boarded up and eventually burned to the ground. The outdoor dance floor was in shambles and of course the trolley line was no longer in operation having been discontinued years earlier. All that remained was the Elmheart Hotel which no longer entertained guests, the ice cream stand, a square dance hall, and the Weidman's.

The round and square dance every other Saturday night was what had really sparked my interest in Manitou Beach. My parents thought the dances were too wild and since I was young would not let me attend. As a typical teenager, I was convinced they had no idea what they were talking about so took matters into my own hands.

One early summer day I heard that Edna was hiring help for the ice cream stand. I convinced Velma, who also wanted a summer job; we should ride our bikes from the cottage to the beach to apply.

To our total surprise (not to mention our parents) Edna hired us both. We were ecstatic! Now that we were gainfully employed every other Saturday night and Sunday afternoons, after a lot of persuasion, our parents agreed to provide transportation. I might add that in no way did we put anything over on them as they saw directly through our plan even mentioning they were not sure either of us was dying to work at an Ice Cream stand especially on Sunday afternoons when all the parties were at the cottages. I had to admit parents could be pretty smart or was it that they were young once too.

The dance began at 9:00 pm and ended at 1:00 am with an intermission at 10:30 which was our busy time. Once the intermission ended we closed the stand finishing about midnight. The first Saturday night my father, who was a marvelous dancer, arrived to pick us up. You can imagine our surprise when he asked if we would like to go to the dance for an hour. I thought I had the best Dad in the world (and I did) as going to the dance for an hour became the routine.

It only took a short period of time for me to realize my infatuation was not just with the dances but with the Elmheart Hotel. George, Edna and I became friends so I spent as much time as possible listening to stories of a time I could only imagine. George, a true character, was at a stand-off until he trusted you. Once he felt comfortable he would relate wonderful tales about the hotel and summers long past. A couple of times they allowed me to roam the hotel where they showed me rooms which had been closed for years.

A room that I particularly liked was the banquet room or large dining room. Old tables and chairs were stacked neatly against the walls however the floor was always freshly swept. The huge room had windows on two sides which allowed a wonderful view of all of the activities on the ever changing lake. I would waltz around the room envisioning pretty women wearing long dresses who with their handsome escort were enjoying a fine dinner. Waiters were scurrying around as they served. Soft music was playing. Once dinner was finished the couple would retreat to the veranda to enjoy the glorious sunset and an after dinner liquor. Edna related stories about the summer activities often mentioning the water slide. There had been long pier which had become a victim of high water. It was not at all unusual for several boats to be docked as the occupants enjoyed the hotel. One day George and I took a walk out to the little grove on the south side of the hotel where he explained that city folks reserved a favorite site returning year after year. The family then pitched a tent and spent their summer vacation in the Grove. I saw pictures of the tents which were mostly white canvas which had been transformed into a true little home away from home. Fishing on the lake and in the bay was great so George made extra money selling bait. Yes, I am positive Manitou Beach was where, had I been born, the place I would have liked to have been.

George and Edna Weidman lived at the Elmheart all of their lives and neither ever married. Years later, following my husband's death, one evening I decided I would like to visit them so I took a drive to the hotel. I entered the bar room and took another step back in time. The room was exactly as I had remembered it years before. Not a single thing had changed.

George dressed in a white shirt and black pants, stood polishing glasses and cleaning the already spotless bar. I looked around quickly realizing I was the only person there. George smiled hello. I asked him where everyone was to which he replied, "They just left."

I smiled as that was a phrase I had heard many times. With that he flipped the bottle opener he had picked up catching it as he turned to ask what I would like. George was a baseball buff and since it was World Series time we discussed the series, my family, and my life. I then asked if I could see Edna. He studied my face for a moment finally announcing he would see and left the room. Soon he reappeared and motioned for me to follow him. We went upstairs to a small living room which had been furnished at least fifty or more years earlier. Edna was sitting staring into space. She turned when I called her name and looked at me, a flicker in her eyes. She smiled but was very quiet; in fact I did all of the talking catching her up on my life. Soon it was time to leave and I did so with a heavy heart. I like to think she knew me. I will never know.

Returning to the bar, I gave George a hug. George was not used to being hugged so the hug was stiff. It was my last visit with the Weidman's. Following their deaths, the Elmheart Hotel sat empty. Every so often I drove to the end of the road to look at the desolate spot. At the time there was talk of condos or a restaurant, however, in the end it was a fire on a cold windy night which left the age old landmark nothing more than a pile of ashes.

And so it was in the hazy, lazy, crazy, days of summers past - a great time to grow up.

THE ELMGROVE GIRLS

Over seventy years ago two young mothers sat sipping ice tea, chatting and watching their baby girls play in a playpen. One of the babies was Carol Mitchell Logan who not only became an artist but she married one when she married Don Logan. The other little child was none other than me, Marilyn Lowden Koss Wright, author of this book.

Three years later a dark haired little girl clutching her doll named Kathy stood on one side of Marilyn Drive while I stood on the other. I asked her name. She announced she was Velma Bridgeman. She then furthered my four year old education by telling when she grew up she was going to be a nurse, get married, have a real baby girl and name her Kathy. So there I thought, I guess she told me! The best part of the story is Velma did exactly that. She became a registered nurse, married John Thiele and when a year later their first daughter arrived they named her Kathy.

A couple of years after Velma moved to the neighborhood the three little girls sat peering through the frosty windows of the school bus as we curiously watched the new girl on the block. The new girl, a little older than we, came slipping and sliding across the icy road. It was no wonder she was having trouble as she was dragging a pair of skis, a musical instrument, a lunch box and a stack of books. Her plight would have been difficult on a good day but this day was snowy and icy.

Little girls are silly. As we watched her struggle we began to giggle uncontrollably. Finally succeeding she collapsed on the seat ahead of us and introduced herself as Joan Vanderbeck. Soon, laughing along with us, she immediately displayed her wonderful sense of humor. She would marry Bill Maier who, with his brother Dick, operated the Maier Farm which was located on Gates-Greece Town Line Road.

By the time we reached school we had become little girls destined to be friends forever. So it was on that frigid winter day that the **Elmgrove Girls** became the **Elmgrove Girls**, a nickname which continues to this day. We were four little girls who grew to womanhood sharing dolls, dreams, secrets and our lives.

Life in our close knit neighborhood located on Elmgrove Road just one mile south of Ridge road was, as described in Patchwork Pieces I, our own version of the Walton's. Carol, Velma and I had brothers; Dick Mitchell, John Bridgeman and Roger Lowden respectively. Marv Hankinson, Gerard and Don Cole, the Meyers, Bud Maggs and later Don Groth completed our age group. We did not have computers, video games, cell phone and for many years no television. However, we did have sand-lot baseball, biking, roller skating and exploring the woods. Winters we went sledding and skating. Often in the spring, Marilyn Drive was the center of the game, Kick the Can. I wonder if kids today would even know that game.

Holidays were special in the neighborhood as all the residents were close friends as well as neighbors. Often there were parties, picnics or some other get together which included everyone. Christmas was, of course, our favorite. As soon as possible on Christmas day we would check with each to see what wonderful gifts we had received. By the way, this was done via the one and only telephone in the house. It could have been coincidence or Santa just knew because many years we each would get a new pair of skates or a new sled. One year everyone got snowshoes. The next day it was off to the pond or hill. Believe it or not once the men left for work we would go sledding on what we called Straub Road Hill. Rarely did a car come down the road until the end of the day. Today, I suspect that even at 3:00 am sledding on Elmgrove road would be totally impossible.

The town of Greece did not have any High Schools until the early sixties. When that milestone arrived we were given a choice of several city of Rochester schools. School days we walked exactly one mile to Ridge road to catch a city bus. Everyone waited for the bus at Red Bornaman's gas station which was located on the corner of Ridge and North Greece road. While waiting at the gas station we widened our friendships to include Herb Gallipeau, George Sheldon and Norm Bissell all of whom lived just west of the gas station on Ridge. Diagonally across Ridge road from the gas station was a diner called Milt and Reds which quickly became a favorite during our high school years.

In no time at all the Elmgrove Girls blossomed into four pretty teenagers which presented a whole new set of problems for our parents as there seemed to be an unending parade of unfamiliar faces to the neighborhood. They appeared in trucks, on motorcycles, or in loud cars which caused my father to exclaim,

"You better tell ….. to slow down and get his muffler fixed."

One evening the Elmgrove girls were at Joan's house when John Maier appeared. John Maier was Bill Maier's cousin. While Bill was often with John this particular night he was not. For a reason I do not remember John fell asleep on the couch. Once we realized John was sleeping we got the bright idea to "borrow" his car which Joan, the only one with a license, could drive. We decided we would drive past Bill Maier's house on Gates Greece Town Line Road. As we cruised by the farm, Joan blew the horn. She meant a friendly tap hello, but as luck would have it, the horn stuck. By this time the Elmgrove girls were laughing hysterically. Joan pulled to the side of the road where we tried to figure out what to do as the horn continued to blare. By this time we had attracted the attention of the entire neighborhood so a nice man came to our rescue. The horn episode took a lot longer than our planned ten minute joy ride. John was awake when we returned and needless to say was not happy with the Elmgrove Girls.

There were many silly incidents during our dating years which we still remember with fondness but as is so true time marched by quickly and it was not long until we each married. Joan was first when she married Bill Maier proving our horn escapade could not scare him away. Carol, Velma and I were still in high school so many days one could find us visiting Joan on the farm. A few years later I married Glenn Koss followed by Velma who married Jack Thiele and later Carol married Don Logan.

Even though we were no longer within walking distance each of us knew there was nothing that would or could break the unwritten law that the Elmgrove Girls never lose touch. There were picnics, dinner parties, lunches, or telephone calls which continue to this day.

Just as is true with many, life has not always been easy for the Elmgrove Girls. In 1987 we lost Velma to cancer. Carol has suffered crippling arthritis for a good share of her adult life although she never complains. Joan still possesses her wonderful sense of humor but she too suffers from arthritis. Each day I give thanks because at the time of this writing my health remains fine. Joan and I lost our sisters as well as Dick Mitchell, John Bridgeman, Don Cole, and Herb Gallipeau.

Recently Joan and Carol came to my cottage for lunch. After they left I began thinking how amazing it is that when we get together the years melt. We are not three elderly women talking about health, instead we become young again as we recall some ridiculous incident of our youth. The Elmgrove Girls raised twelve children, lots of grandchildren and Joan ahead of us once again, is a great grandmother.

Often I drive Elmgrove road which is a back route to the Greece mall. While our portion of Elmgrove road is still a neighborhood, the neighborhood we remember no longer exists. Our parents, grandparents, aunts, uncles and neighbors are gone with the exception of how vividly I see them in my mind. Passing Joan's house first, I see Eleanor Vanderbeck waving at me. Next I smell the unmistakable smell of a fireplace fire which mom has started to remove the chill. I note a gang of boys playing touch football in the yard. I see Velma's mother, Jessie Bridgeman pulling into her driveway as she returns from a day of teaching at Greece Central. My precious Nan is on her porch hollering for me to bring the girls in for cookies and finally I see Jessie Mitchell, Carol's mother, reminding me to be careful not to hit the tree as I back out of their yard.

Yes, we grew up in a special time, in a special place and I know that I speak not only for the Elmgrove girls, but for all of us fortunate enough to have been there. If we could, I know each one of us would do it all again!!

HISTORIC RIDGE ROAD - ROUTE 104

Writing a book of local history would not be complete if I were not to write my memories of Ridge Road, Route 104. The road stretches from Niagara Falls across much of New York State; however, my memories consist of a few miles of highway between Manitou Road, Greece NY and Lake Avenue in the city of Rochester.

Within the last year, I was driving east on Ridge Road toward Rochester when I approached the traffic light at Long Pond and Ridge. Once stopped, I glanced to the left I where I noted a huge bulldozer smashing into what used to be Buckman's Dairy. The destruction of Buckman's Dairy caught me by surprise. I was saddened by the sight knowing full well it was progress striking again. My thought immediately was confirmed as I read a large sign boasting 'Future Home of Walgreens.' Great, I thought, we really need another drugstore. The wonderful smells of baked goods, the yummy donuts and the homemade ice cream nothing more than a memory.

I watched totally mesmerized until horns blasting jarred me back to reality. Based upon the general public's reaction, I guessed they cared far less than I that Buckman's Dairy was being knocked to nothing. Realizing I must do something, rather than continuing on my journey, I made a right turn on Long Pond Road followed by a quick left into the parking lot of Ruby Tuesday's. There I was able to observe the destruction while recalling my thoughts of what once was the "hub" of the town of Greece. As I did so, I wished Charles Peterson, a master artist in ghost paintings, could be sitting with me as I described the block as I remembered it. My car was parked where the Grange Hall building was once located.

Looking west across Long Pond Road I noted Heritage Jewelers. In my day that building was a Red & White grocery store owned by Ray and Mary Craft who were also our neighbors on Alder Beach. As I thought about the grocery store, it brought to mind another fond memory of my grandmother.

My mother's mother, I called her Nan. Nan would call me in the afternoon to ask if I wanted to ride with her to pick up Gramps from work. Gramps (Roy Cole) was the building inspector for the town of Greece with his office located in the Greece Town Hall which before its demise would have been directly behind my current parking spot. Nan, who lived just five houses south on Elmgrove would pick me up, then drive north on Elmgrove Road just out of my mother's sight, should she be watching, where she stopped the car. She would then let me drive. We would proceed north to Ridge turn right and continue to the very corner I was now observing. As we approached Long Pond Road, Nan would tell me to pull far to the right in the Red & White parking lot where we changed drivers again. Nan knew everyone so she was always waving and hollering hello. It did not seem to bother her, other than my mother or grandfather finding out, that I did not have a permit much less a license and in reality I am not sure she had one either. Of course, I loved the trip making it with her as often as I could.

Nan would then proceed to drive the car across Long Pond Road where she would pull into the front drive of the Greece Town Hall to wait for Grandpa. As I thought about our wait for Grandpa, I glanced behind me at the modern building housing Pier One and Ruby Tuesdays. Magically those buildings disappeared and in their place stood the stately Greece Town Hall. Almost every community event was held at the Town Hall. I remember dance recitals, minstrel shows, queen contests, youth dances and all sorts of events. The building had wide sweeping front steps. On the second floor there were octagon windows located on either side of the door. Grandpa's office was behind one of them. The building had a beautiful cupola which is now located in front of the Historical Society on Long Pond Road.

Looking directly across Ridge Road from where I was sitting, I envisioned the beautiful fieldstone church which was the Greece Baptist church. It was a wonderful old building with a parsonage to the east on the Ridge. The church was torn down in the fifties and replaced with a building further down on Long Pond road. I grew up in Greece Baptist church and as I sat there I recalled the Saturday mornings our youth group gathered at the church. A young man from West Virginia studying to be a minister was in charge of us. I am confident he was delighted when the weekly session ended as in addition to not always paying attention, we would beg him to let us go to Buckman's for donuts. After much persuasion and probably just to shut us up, he would let a couple of us march across the road for the still warm delicacies. Thinking about that made me wonder whatever happened to Rich Fitch, the young man who tried so hard to teach us Christianity. We certainly tested his.

Just west of Buckman's was a row of houses in which one of grandpa's brothers lived. The lovely home belonging to George Saunders, MD was located just in front of the houses. An electric company was among several businesses later located in Dr. Saunder's home, however, now the stately home has been demolished as well.

Realizing it was time for me to continue on my errand, I drove out of the parking lot turning left on Long Pond now a one way street. I proceeded to the mall to turn around and pulled onto the Long Pond Road extension which used to be named Mitchell Road. Wow, remember when there was no Greece Town Mall? I certainly do. In its place was a development of post-war bungalows. On the Ridge there was a general store, a tavern, and Whitman's Garage all within walking distance. Hein's Diner, later Naum's Diner, was located approximately where Party City is today. St. John's Church, another magnificent building now boarded up. Remembering the few times I attended the beautiful church with Velma I recalled the stunning stained glass windows and I also thought about my fascination with the Stations of the Cross.

As I drove east I passed the century old Falls Cemetery now the resting place of many early settlers of Greece. Passing the cemetery caused me to think about the huge Memorial Day parades of my youth. The parade originated at the town hall and ended at the cemetery with a regal ceremony for our fallen heroes. Having twirled baton in a few parades, I could not help but wonder what some would think if they could see the super highway today. Lovely Victorian homes have been replaced by restaurants, professional offices, and interstate ramps.

The light turned red at Hoover Drive which gave me a chance to glance at the Greece Central School Building. The building, now getting old, is special to me as it was my elementary school. The light turned green and I resumed my trip. I drove past an area which we called Koda-Vista. Homes flourished in Koda-Vista following World War II. The name is pretty obvious as the Eastman Kodak Company was the largest employer in the area. Every family had someone working at the big 'yellow box.' Kodak put Rochester, NY on the map as it was world renowned. Never did I dream we would see that company go into bankruptcy. As I continued to think about Eastman Kodak, another casualty of our modern world, I suddenly realized it was time for me to ease into the new turning lane which would take me to my destination.

Waiting to turn I looked to my right and noted the old parking of VerHults Farm Market. Just down the road Mike Conroy's restaurant was once located. It was an upscale restaurant so if one was going to Mike Conroy's for dinner the event measured right up with going to the Crescent Beach Hotel. People did not go out for dinner as they do today so if you were going to dinner at either of those restaurants the event usually signaled something very important was happening in your life.

I parked in front of Staples Office Supply thoughtfully continuing my trip down memory lane thinking about 'the end of the Ridge.' I began to wonder where the nickname originated since the four corners of Dewey Avenue and Ridge Road were not even close to the end of the road. However, it is the name which I have known forever and which I still use. The block flourished with successful businesses as in a jewelry store, Neisiner's, Sears, the White Tower, one of the early Wegman grocery stores and many others. One of my first jobs was as a cashier at that particular Wegman's store. Believe it or not we actually had to figure, in our heads, the cost of a can of vegetables if the price was three for a dollar. When work was finished I walked to the Dewey Terminal where I caught the last bus to Elmgrove road. As I recall that bus on weekdays ran at 5:30 pm.

My errand at Staples completed, I returned home retracing the route to Manitou Road via Ridge Road. As I did so I counted not one, not two, not three, but at least six car lots. Driving past Sam's plaza I recalled Grandpa Cole remarking that no one would ever be able to build in that location because it was so low and water would be a problem. Wouldn't he be surprised?

The driveway leading into Kohl's Department Store was the approximate location of the Lyon's Den Bowling Hall. Owners, Gene & Betty Lyons, were friends of my parents. I bet there are many men around who as boys set pins at the Lyons Den or bowled in one of the leagues.

Streb's Restaurant is the next business one passes that is no longer in existence. The windows are boarded and there is a large sign nailed to the front of the building indicating the building is for sale. The parking lot was packed full of cars though. There were at least twenty new cars which belong to the car dealer next door.

I noted the little cobblestone house on the north side of the road just east of Streb's. It has orange fencing around it so I am hoping that means that it is not slated for demolition. There is a story I have heard since childhood about a man who lived in the cobblestone many years ago. Folklore has it that the man spent his days sitting on the porch watching the world go by. From time to time the local doctor who travelled to a house call in his horse and carriage would gallop by. The old man would holler, "Hoosick?" "Hoosick?" Supposedly it is how Hoosick Cemetery at Manitou and Ridge got its name.

A final Ridge Road story I would like to share is one of my Mom's. Mom, five at the time, was with my grandparents as they travelled home from a grange meeting during a snowstorm. In a horse drawn sleigh they were just about in front of North Avenue when one of those newfangled things called a car came along. The car made so much noise it spooked the horse causing the horse to rear in the air and the sleigh tipped over in the snow. Everyone was shaken and thankfully no one was hurt.

True to the times, along came another sleigh. The men were able to upright my grandparents sleigh, quiet the horse, and they continued home but the memory remained vivid to my mother. By the way, the car kept right on going!

Ridge Road will be Ridge Road forever that much I know. Perhaps in another fifty years another will write their memories of changes along the road, although I have no idea what could possibly be as dramatic... perhaps more car lots? Better yet, perhaps one day it will be an eight lane highway with extra turning lanes.

GREECE CENTRAL SCHOOL

"By the old historic Ridge Road, stands our district's pride, dearer to our sons and daughters than all else besides....Greece Central, Greece Central" and on the song goes. These words are the first line of my grammar schools alma mater, Greece Central School, located on Hoover Drive

When one is barely five years old getting on a large yellow bus to head off anywhere is overwhelming. It was a help that all of the neighborhood kids were on the same bus as there were only a couple of buses for the entire town.

The good news, although I did not think so at all, was that my brother, Roger, two years my senior had been put in strict charge of me, a job which he took to heart. He delivered me to my kindergarten class where I was instructed not to dare leave until he returned to drag me home. Looking back my mother definitely knew what she was doing as I could get lost in the kindergarten room much less find my way home so waiting for my brother turned out to be ok.

I find it strange as I put a memory to pen the vivid reality with which I remember certain things almost as if I were sitting in the room again. For instance, I remember children sitting on the waste basket. For the life of me I cannot remember why that would have happened, but I remember it.

At Greece Central many friendships were created many of which are still in place. It was there that I met Sue Kenyon, Ruth Shaw, Steve Carter, Henry Coates, Myron Easton, Sylvia Osborne, Nancy Stahl, Richard Schlosser and Sue Stutzman to mention just a few. In fact we knew everyone in school not necessarily just our class but other classes as well.

Ruthie Shaw was a red headed, freckled face, vivacious little girl who as a grown woman died far too young of breast cancer. Ruth was married, the mother of six sons, and a teacher in Hilton in the elementary building where I was a secretary in 1978 when my husband Glenn died. Shortly thereafter Ruth invited me for dinner. As we sat reminiscing about Greece Central and our childhood she told me a wonderful story about Christmas of our Kindergarten year.

Ruth's mother asked what she wanted for Christmas. Ruth replied she wanted a pair of glasses just like Marilyn Lowden wore. A minute later she added she also wanted a red purse just like Marilyn Lowden had so she could put her glasses in the purse, just the way that Marilyn Lowden did.

Her story made me laugh out loud, not only at how funny it was, but because as a little girl, my left eye was diagnosed as a lazy eye. The eye turned in making one look cross-eyed. Surgery for a lazy eye was unheard of in the forties and the prescribed treatment was to cover the good eye with a rubber patch to strengthen the bad eye. The rubber patch dug into my face, making a ring which resembled a raccoon and the patch itched. The itching not only made me cry but when tears dripped onto my face they created a sweaty mess. I HATED MY GLASSES AND MORE THAN THAT, I HATED THE DISPICABLE RUBBER PATCH!

Just as soon as I was out of my mother's sight my glasses were deposited into my little red purse. Little did I know that my mother pinned a note to my sweater which read, 'If you see this little girl without her glasses, tell her to put them on.'

Ruthie got her red purse for Christmas, however, by the time in our lives we re-lived our kindergarten year, both of us were avoiding glasses like the plague. It was a great memory though. By the way, the treatment on my lazy eye did succeed. Thank goodness.

The graduating class of 1950 had perhaps sixty youngsters all of whom we knew well. Sometime after kindergarten, we were split into two groups of the alphabet. One group consisted of last names which began A-L and the other M-Z. During our sixth grade year departmentalization was implemented so after Christmas vacation we began to change classrooms for certain subjects. In order to balance the classes those of us who had a last name which began with L were switched to the end of the alphabet which now became L-Z. To tell you the truth I was devastated for a few days as I passed my A-K friends in the hall and I would sadly wave at them. Kids are resilient and before long we all adjusted just fine. After all, we were all together at lunch and in gym so it was ok.

Valentine's Day arrived and as we passed classes in the hall, a C slipped a little package into my hand. I could not wait to open that package. Inside the box was the tackiest pin ever to have been made. About two inches long, the pin was an oriental man wearing a round hat. The finish of the pin was a silver color paper which kept flaking thereby leaving a black spot. None of that mattered as I thought it was the hope diamond. I wore the pin everywhere as it was first gift I ever received from a boy.

As I write the class of 1950 who were so full of hopes and dreams are now on the downside of the circle. We know all too well, while it seems impossible, our lives are quickly passing. All that being said there is something on which I would bet my Social Security check. Greece Central School, its teachers, along with every member of our class will never be forgotten.

When we graduated from 8th grade in 1950 with no high schools in Greece, we were sent to Rochester. We were given choices such as John Marshall, Charlotte, Edison, Nazareth, Aquinas, however, I wanted to go to Spencerport. The Spencerport district line was ten houses south of my house with the cost of transportation being ninety dollars a year. My parents could not afford ninety dollars a year for transportation which was already paid if I went to a city school. I went to John Marshall High School, a decision which turned out to be another excellent thread of my life as not only did it open many horizons but it widened my circle of friends.

Mom used to say, "Make new friends, but keep the old! These are silver, those are gold!" As always - Mom was right!

Editor's note: The Democrat and Chronicle reported in December, 2012 that the Greece Central School building, aka Odyssey School has been sold.

NELLIE'S GLOBE

Nellie Chase Lewis was my paternal great-grandmother. My father Homer, the oldest of four boys, was extremely fond of his grandmother. She was the woman who had our Alder Beach cottage built, something for which I shall always be thankful; often wishing I had had the opportunity to meet her.

Cottages in 1927 were pretty simple in that the downstairs was a large room with a porch separated by French doors. The large living room resembled a studio apartment. On one side of the room there was a make-shift kitchen with a sink and simple cupboards covered with fabric curtains. The other side of the room held white wicker furniture, a wind-up RCA record player with a big horn on the top. One corner had a rustic cupboard in which all sorts of interesting stuff had been stored and eventually forgotten. The cupboard contained dishes, games, oil lamps, even a jar of colorful sea glass. Among the souvenirs was a white satin glass globe decorated with delicate hand painted pink flowers. The globe was the top of a Gone with the Wind oil lamp the bottom of which had been broken years earlier.

Even though the cottage had been remodeled and redecorated several times the corner cupboard remained untouched. By the late sixties, my family was spending summers at the cottage so little by little I was making my own changes. One rainy day, I decided to clean the rustic corner cupboard. I examined each item deciding its fate when I came upon the white satin glass globe. Because I knew that Dad treasured his grandmother's globe and it was so pretty I decided I would take it to my home for safe keeping. At my home, I carefully placed the globe on the top shelf of a kitchen cupboard. From time to time I would glance at the globe trying to decide how to incorporate it into my then extremely contemporary décor. It just did not seem to fit.

Several years passed when I found myself hosting an estate sale at our home because Glenn had inherited a small house full of antiques. Due to the location we were unable to have the sale at the house so we transported everything to our house. At the same time we were invited by friends to take a trip to Aruba. We really wanted to go so we agreed the profits from sale would take us on a second honeymoon for our twentieth anniversary.

The sale became so large that we opened the family room as well as the garage, yard and porch. Several friends helped while I handled the money in the kitchen. Waiting to pay for her purchases an elderly woman spied Grandmother Nellie's globe through the open cupboard door. She asked its price. I told her it was not for sale. Persisting, she told me she collected lamps and explained that it was extremely hard to find an original satin glass globe in good condition. She then offered me fifty dollars. The balmy winds of Aruba were calling. Fifty dollars was a lot of money. I quickly reasoned Dad had given me the globe so he probably wouldn't care if I sold it. As I took the money, I remarked that the globe had belonged to my great-grandmother and even remarked I was not sure if I should sell it. However within minutes the elderly lady was out the door with Nellie's globe and I had fifty dollars.

Our father, a handsome, gentle, man loved us unconditionally rarely becoming angry. While Dad would never tolerate foul language from his girls, his language could be fairly colorful. Occasionally he used the lord's name in vain in a statement which began, "J …. C…… what were you thinking?"

It was just such a day when casually I mentioned I sold the globe. He was obviously very angry with me as he asked the price. He then announced if I wanted fifty dollars I should have asked him. There is not an adjective which would describe my feelings, but it was too late, the globe was gone. For a long time I wondered about the lady hoping perhaps I would run into her. I never did. Within days, Dad forgave me, but the haunting feeling of what I had done never left. I was truly sorry.

Glenn and I went to Aruba that winter. It was a wonderful trip and the last trip we would ever take as he died of cancer a year and a half later. Dad passed with emphysema in 1985.

Twenty-four years passed since I had sold Nellie's globe. On a lovely fall morning in 1999 I was drinking coffee when I glanced out the window to see a little old lady struggling to walk up the driveway. It was obvious she was having difficulty breathing so I opened the door to ask if I could help. As she moved closer I realized it was the lady who bought Nellie's globe. I could not imagine why she was there other than to ask what I had for sale as I had recently opened a small business as an Antique and Collectible dealer.

Approaching the porch, she asked if I remembered her. I nodded yes and invited her in. In the next few minutes she revealed her husband had recently died so she was moving to an apartment. She then told me she recalled how hesitant I was to sell her Nellie's globe including that Nellie was my great-grandmother. I was nodding yes, then shared that Dad was very unhappy with me.

Smiling, she asked if I would like to buy Nellie's globe back. Not believing what I had just heard, I jumped up to find my checkbook. I did not care what she wanted to charge for the globe so I was amazed when she said she would like $60.00. That was just $10.00 more than what she paid. Again there are no adjectives which would describe my feelings other than I was thrilled beyond words.

Mrs. Frisbee then told me that she had made up her mind the day she bought the globe that one day she would bring it back. She said when she told her husband her wishes he surprised her when he told her he was a distant relative of my father's. I was also very surprised.

I helped her walk to her car where I found Nellie's globe carefully packed in a box of packing bubble. The globe was in perfect shape. We both had tears in our eyes as we hugged when she left. The whole episode was unbelievable.

I returned to the house and carefully placed my great-grandmother's globe where I could just look at it as I tried to decide upon a truly special place for it in my home. Suddenly, almost as though I was being told, the idea that the globe would make a wonderful pendant light jumped into my mind. That very afternoon I went to a shop specializing in antique lamps where I had the light made. When it was completed, I had the pendant light installed in a corner window over my kitchen sink.

Each day as darkness falls, I turn on Nellie's globe. The globe is gorgeous wicker white ball with delicate pink flowers hand painted strategically in several spots. Once lit the globe reminds one of a lovely full moon. Call me crazy, but I often feel my father's arm as he gives my shoulders a hug.

My great-grandmother Nellie's globe is home where it belongs.

THE GOODBYE MEMORY

It was almost March 2, my sister Lonna's birthday. I found myself wandering aimlessly through one of our favorite stores as I searched for a gift. I paused to squirt a perfume tester. As I savored the delicate scent of flowers I pondered on the pretty perfume. No, perfume would not do, nor would a scarf or jewelry. Each item I picked up I rejected quickly as Lonna was gravely ill.

I stopped walking for a moment hoping for an inspiration and I recalled that just a few days earlier Lonna mentioned the comfort she felt by surrounding herself with beautiful things. She explained that it seemed to allow her to escape her illness for even a few minutes as she thought about the object she was enjoying. The idea of perhaps a lovely painting or a pretty springtime centerpiece jumped into my thoughts. Pleased with the idea I resumed my search as I headed for the home décor department located at the rear of the building.

As I walked quickly through the store I glanced from side to side observing the lovely new spring merchandise when suddenly a lovely handbag caught my eye. Since handbags are a passion of mine I stopped to stare at the bag. It was a gorgeous shade of aqua blue-green. The mannequin was dressed in the latest style of a casual rain coat with the bag slung over her shoulder. It instantly gave the impression the woman was about to go out for lunch or do some errands.

The handbag was large with several compartments. I even noted a pocket for a cell phone. As I examined the handbag, I thought about the many times Lonna had teased me about losing my keys in some giant handbag. Just a few days before, during one of several hospitalizations, she had pointed to the bag I was carrying as she announced to her daughters that I never carried the same purse more than a day. She then asked if I knew where my keys were. I searched forever and finally produced the large keychain. We all laughed. That settled it, my decision was made. I bought the handbag.

As I wrapped her present, I second guessed myself. Perhaps this was not the best gift after all, as Lonna was rarely out of bed for long periods of time. However, if anyone inquired as to how she was feeling she always responded with a smile and would say,

"I'm fine," followed by, "Let's talk about something else." and we would.

March 2nd arrived with more than a hint of spring in 2006 and it was a bright sunny day when I arrived for our visit. Lonna was sitting in her family room and looked lovely. A beautiful, talented woman, the chemotherapy had left her artistic hands numb, however that day she had managed her make-up and hair perfectly. On the couch nestled close to her was her beloved dog, Buddy.

We were never good at waiting to open presents so when I gave her my gift, she grabbed the present and tore off the paper in a childlike manner revealing the beautiful handbag. She looked at the bag and then at me. I saw the look of total surprise and pure joy in her eyes. I instantly knew I had made the right choice. Lonna LOVED the handbag. As she examined each nook and cranny she asked me to find her old handbag.

With the sun warming our backs we sat on the couch as she changed her belongings from the old purse to the new one. We chatted incessantly about the kids, the weather, and the local gossip. When she was finished, Lonna patted the handbag mentioning again how much she liked the bag.

We had fun that lovely spring day as we laughed and joked. After a couple of hours, I noted her beginning to tire so knew it was time to leave. I was determined, as was she, to simply say Happy Birthday. I managed to get into my car before the tears came as I knew in my heart, my younger sister who was also my best friend, was celebrating her last birthday on this earth.

Later that evening, Lonna called to tell me the handbag was her favorite gift. She said I had touched her heart. Neither of us wanted to hang up the telephone so we talked for hours.

A few days later, following a doctor visit, she quipped, "Well I finally got to go somewhere with my new handbag." The handbag was in the hospital room when she passed.

It has been several years since that March day, in fact as I write March 2 is just around the corner. I have thought many times about that last birthday celebration. Having shared all of our birthdays, many memorable, one that I shall always cherish is the Goodbye Memory. The lesson I learned is undying love which surpasses all understanding.

It has been several years today,
Those we love do not go away,
They walk beside us every day.
Unseen, unheard, but always near,
So loved, so missed and so very dear,
Loved forever and ever!

(Author unknown)

In memory of Lonna Jacquelyn Lowden DeRoo

MY BABY SISTER

By

Paige Southwell Koss

My life had always been calm until I got my little baby sister. Now, everything is moving and hectic.

It was a beautiful spring day when my sister came home. She weighed two pounds when she was born on March 18, 2008. We had to wait two months before she could come home. Everything was ready for the little gift from God. Her bed was cozy and ready to go. Her toys had been bought (after much research on which ones to get for her) and all of our hearts had a spot for her. From the first moment I laid my hand on the soft surface of her head, I knew she was ours.

On that spring day, I thought about what my mother had said so many times before. "She picked us, we did not pick her." I realized that day that she wasn't the kind of sister everyone hated. In fact, the first thing everyone wants to do when they come to my house is play with her. At first that perplexed me, but now I know I can't resist her either. She is always the center of attention, but I knew when she arrived it would be different. Boy is it ever!

There has always been the pitter patter of little feet in our house since she was born. "Feed the baby" and "Don't tease her" Boy does that get on my nerves. If the smallest thing is wrong with her it's - "oh, take her to the Doctor." Yet when my stomach hurts my parents tell me "Go lay down." Another thing that annoys me is that when she does something wrong my parents say "Oh that's ok baby" or "Paige can you clean that up?" UGH!

Sometimes though, some magic everyday thing will happen and I will forget about everything. Like when she comes to me with that cute face and wants me to play. Or when she hops up on my lap and snuggles with me. Those moments make me remember how I felt on that spring day in 2008. When those moments happen I store them in my mind and realize that when I am older and she is gone, I'll miss her.

That little sister, Cookie Lyn, is the cutest little Yorkshire terrier I have ever seen. She always brightens my day when I come home. When she looks at me with those beautiful eyes I think back to that spring and just accept that however many mistakes she makes she will always be a part of my family.

Editor's note: Paige, my granddaughter, was upset with a homework assignment and was relating her annoyance to me.

The assignment was as follows: Everyone has a place in a family. You may be the oldest or the youngest or perhaps in the middle. How does this affect your everyday life? Write a narrative giving a snapshot of what it is like to be in your place.

Paige is an only child which was the reason she was annoyed. I suggested to her that she let her creative juices flow with this story being the result.

Unedited, I wanted to include the story exactly as it was written by a little girl ten years old. I might be biased however I see another author in our family. What do you think?

THE LOWDEN TOMAHAWK

Picture, if you will that you are sitting in a cabin or farm house some two hundred years ago. Try to imagine what you would see as you looked out a window. I don't believe you would have seen paved roads, telephone poles or electric lines. Most likely you would be looking into a forest of trees where just enough timber had been cleared for your primitive home and the road would be nothing more than a trodden lane. Perhaps your family would have been fortunate enough to settle on the shores of a lake or pond as was the case for my father's branch of the Lowden family.

My seventh great-grandfather, Jacob traveled with his family, as well as his brother's family to homestead a farm which was bordered by what is known as Long Pond here in New York State. Jacob was a Veteran of the War of 1812. There was a wagon trail which passed through the farm which was later officially named Lowden Point Road. Lowden Point Road runs from Edgemere Drive to Frisbee Hill Road in the Town of Greece, NY. If one were to travel east on Frisbee Hill Road to the end of the road and make a left hand turn you would be on Lowden Point Road. Approximately a mile down the road on the right hand side of the road there is a small cemetery which is the Lowden family cemetery. The cemetery is the resting place of our ever so great-grandparents, Jacob and Sarah along with several of their children. Jacob's brother William and his wife are also buried there.

History tells us diseases flew through wilderness settlements often killing everyone in its path. Our grandparents lost three children overnight, an infant and two toddlers. One of the children who died that night was a little girl named Nancy, age one. Nancy was born on September 2, 1820. Oddly enough I was born on September 2, almost one hundred and twenty years later.

To say life was difficult sounds trite as when one thinks about the hardships people endured. The thought of losing one child is unthinkable much less three little ones. I cannot believe the strength of our ancestors. Somehow they accepted and took life as it was. I suspect if we were able to visit with them they would tell us that for the most part life had treated them well. They had a home, food, a farm and most importantly a family. I recall someone dear to me expressing the thought that no one ever told them life would be easy and it wasn't.

The Lowden homestead was built across the road from the cemetery where several generations of Lowden's resided until the land was sold. They, like many settlers, were farmers.

Our ever so great-grandfather was a fair and peaceful man so when a group of Seneca Indians travelled the Cattaraugus trail to the shores of Long Pond hoping to fish he allowed them to set- up camp for a few days each year. One year winter came early in the form of an unexpected severe snowstorm. The snow was so deep the Indians could not leave. Jacob told them they could remain as long as needed which turned into a few weeks. Jacob's wife, Sarah, was not happy with his decision. Sarah, working in her kitchen would look out the window from time to time only to see an Indian staring at her. Jacob told her the Indians would not harm them, but Sarah did not believe him. She did not, nor would she allow her children, to venture far from the house.

Finally there was enough of a winter thaw to allow the Indians to return home which was in the Avon, NY area. As a thank-you to Jacob the Indians gave him a parting gift of an Indian tomahawk. The tomahawk has a long hollow wooden handle and is also a peace pipe. According to experts in the field, the head of the tomahawk which is etched metal was most likely an item for which the Indians had traded fur pelts. While there is no record that the pipe was ever passed around as an offering of peace, the tomahawk is a true treasure.

For the last several years when the fourth grades at the Village Elementary School in Hilton are studying Indians, a few of us connected with the Parma Historical Society do a presentation for the students. For my part of the presentation I take the tomahawk and relate the story of its origin.

The Lowden home including barns was torn down many years ago. Today the shores of Long Pond are dotted with several hundred homes. However, whenever I visit the family plot I try to imagine life as it was all those years ago. My eyes scour the shores of the pond trying to envision a little Indian village and what it might have looked like during that harsh winter. I see myself working in the kitchen of the house and I glance out the window only to see an Indian peering back at me. What would I do? I know without a doubt I would do exactly as my Grandmother Sarah only perhaps much more vocal.

Editor's note: In recent years, in conjunction with the Town of Greece, my nephew, Steven Lowden worked diligently to restore and preserve the Lowden Cemetery as the cemetery is a historical site. Thanks to all who had a hand in accomplishing the project.

The members of the Lowden family are extremely proud of our heritage and of our ever so great-grandfather, Jacob, a Veteran of the War of 1812 and a pioneer settler of the town of Greece, NY.

MIKE ADAMS' GARAGE
A TRIBUTE TO CABIC & BADGE
FORD DEALERSHIP

Franklin Adams, better known as 'Mike' is a quiet, unassuming man who had a dream he has brought to reality. As a young man, Mike developed a love of the Ford Motor Company which has never diminished. That coupled with the hobby of restoring antique cars spurred him on to wanting to build his own state of the art garage including the idea of dedicating the garage to a couple of guys who contributed to the history of both Greece and Parma having owned Ford dealerships.

Cabic & Badge first opened their doors in 1931 at 3570 Latta Road in North Greece. The dealership owned by Ed Cabic and Ray Badge flourished for over thirty years in a building which consisted of a small showroom, an office, a parts room and a workshop at the rear of the building. The Cabic & Badge business became well known throughout the local NY area for their high quality service and workmanship.

The friendly atmosphere was the social event of the day as men waited for repairs to be done. Mike smiled as he recalled taking his 1957 Ford to the dealership for inspection. Suddenly, the fire whistle blew. Since the men were all volunteer firemen, they dropped their wrenches and ran. Dashing by Mike who was in the waiting room they hollered,

"Don't forget to close the door when you leave." There was no car inspection to be done that day and as Mike said, no one seemed to mind.

In 1964, Cabic & Badge dealership on Latta Road closed with Ray Badge re-opening at a new location on Lake Avenue in Hilton, NY. Badge Motors operated at that location from 1964 until 1971.

It was during that time that Mike had an opportunity to work with several men he admired. Names, familiar, to the area such as Ken Speer, Dave Griffin, Bill Stark and Dave Quinn were tossed around as Mike recalled his memories during our interview.

One story which I particularly liked was how often in the very early spring, it was not unusual for the men to arrive at work to see that several farm trucks had made their way to the garage for their annual tune-up. Several months later those same farm trucks, often before daybreak, had dropped off bushels of luscious produce for the workers to enjoy. Those truly were the good old days.

In 2006, Mike's son, David, built his Dad's dream garage behind their home in Parma and true to his word; Mike dedicated the garage to Cabic & Badge. When one enters the spotless building, aside from all the modern day tools, time stands still. The building is filled with tools and memorabilia acquired from gas stations or dealerships now closed. Many of the items have come from family and friends and Mike delights in relating the origin of each.

As one glances throughout the shop in Mike's garage one expects to see Ed Cabic, his corn cob pipe in tow. Or perhaps Ray 'Bub' Badge, Ken 'Senator' Speer, or Dave Quinn will stick their heads out from under a hood asking if they can help you. Time truly stands still!

Although the original Cabic & Badge dealership never owned a tow truck, a couple of years ago, Mike bought a Model A pick-up and restored it to what he thought the men would have liked. It is a total creation of love and dedication to a couple of guys who crossed Mike's path as a young man and made a difference in his life.

Franklin and Ann, who prefer to be called "Mike and Rocky" are life-long residents of Parma and as of this writing belong to many antique car clubs. Mike has brilliantly restored several cars receiving national recognition through magazine articles, one cover of which featured his 1937 Ford Station Wagon, commonly called a "Woodie."

One can see Mike's cars at the various shows, particularly the Hilton Applefest, where it is not the least unusual for him to take several blue ribbons.

It is my thought that if one has a dream, they should never let it go. Mike Adams is living proof that my thought is true.

Editor's note: My father, Homer (Jack) Lowden was a faithful patron of Cabic & Badge. When I was eight years old, Dad returned from a service visit at their shop where he had purchased a gift for me. Cabic & Badge were replacing their typewriter so Dad bought the old Underwood for $5.00. The typewriter was the start of my writing career. How I wish I had kept that old machine as I know it would have a revered spot in Mike Adam's garage.

374 BENNETT ROAD IS SAVED

(Was it divine intervention?)

Bennett Road is a country road which runs north and south between Huffer Road and Wilder road in the town of Parma, NY. Just south of Curtis road on the East side of the creek there is a grey farm house close to the road which is 374 Bennett Road. It is the house where my first husband, Glenn Koss was raised. The house owned by his paternal grandparents housed the entire family. Glenn, his parents, brother as well as his grandparents lived there.

The property is a lovely parcel of land consisting of a couple of acres which border the creek. Glenn's grandmother loved flowers and growing plants, so much so that she had two greenhouses built in the 1940's where she began her florist business, Koss Florist. Glenn inherited his grandmother's love of horticulture and it became his dream to one day own and operate a full-fledged nursery. He graduated from Alfred School of Horticulture during the Korean conflict; thus his dream had to be put on hold while he served in the Air Force. It was following his four year stint in the service when we fell in love and married.

Glenn, a handsome, quiet man was multi-talented. So while horticulture was his first love during his years in the service he had become a mechanic. Since the business would take time to grow and bills had to be paid, Glenn took a job in the Hilton School District as a Bus Mechanic. Nights and weekends we worked to get the florist and nursery business off the ground. The business was growing however, in the early sixties our lives took one of those unexpected turns.

Shortly after our first son was born, Glenn was diagnosed with a lung disease similar to coal miner's black lung, called sarcoid. It is a disease, which at the time, was offered little help except taking steroids. Since the furnace at the greenhouse was coal fired, the recommendation was the greenhouses had to be closed. Glenn's dream ended although he continued to grow plants until his untimely death resulting from a cancer which was directly related to the sarcoid.

Florence, Glenn's mother, was a strong German woman whose own life had been anything but easy, lived on Bennett Road until her passing. She had come to the property as a young woman and had raised her family there. Flossie truly loved her home announcing to all in no uncertain terms that she had no intention of leaving there until the time came that she must.

A few weeks after her death in 1987, both of my sons received letters from the lawyer indicating Florence had changed her will sometime earlier leaving her entire estate to Glenn's only brother who lived in Colorado. The estate consisted almost solely of the Bennett Road property. When I read the letter, to be perfectly honest, I was disappointed for my sons as both had spent much of their lives with their father at Bennett road. They knew of his love of the property as well as it was the last link to their dad and their grandmother. In addition, the thought had been that perhaps one of them would be able to purchase the property, thus keeping it in the family.

Florence, Flossie as I called her, was a marvelous woman, a super mother-in-law, and a wonderful grandmother. She adored her grandsons so that while it may have been slightly difficult for them to understand at the time, they accepted her decision knowing she loved them deeply and would never hurt them intentionally.

For several years the house was rented. Then one summer as I drove the road daily, I noted there was work being done on the property. This was followed by a "For Sale" sign in the yard. Seeing the sign took us by surprise and we all felt extremely sad. The property had been in the Koss family for a generation and now was being sold.

A month or so later I returned home one evening to observe a call on my answering machine from my lawyer. My lawyer was also my brother-in-law's attorney. The message asked me to return his call as he wanted to "pick my brain" regarding 374 Bennett Road. Since I had no interest in helping with the sale of the property and we were going out of town for the weekend I decided I would call upon my return.

When we returned the lawyer had left a second message. This time he announced he would like me to call him as soon as possible to discuss my possible "interest" in 374 Bennett Road.

This message got my immediate attention so I called the attorney, John Foster. John explained that my brother-in-law had sold the property to a neighbor and that the closing was scheduled for three days. He then quizzed me on the passing of my husband, as well as my father-in-law, only to reveal the amazing news that per the laws when both those men passed, I owned one-sixth of the property. Someone could have knocked me over with a feather.

When I caught my breath, I asked him what one-sixth I owned. I thought perhaps my one-sixth was a small portion of the wooded creek. Not so my lawyer informed me, I owned one-sixth of the entire property.

"Can I refuse to sell?" I asked.

"Yes!" he answered. However, he explained on behalf of his client they were asking me to sign-off the property and at closing, I would receive one-sixth of the final sale. In less than ten seconds, I replied, "Please inform your client, I will not sign off on the Bennett Road property."

For a second there was complete silence and then John said he would inform his client explaining to me that he could not represent us both at the same time which I understood completely.

Often in my writing I try to describe emotions in a given situation. This particular time there are no words that I can think of which would truly describe my feelings. Disbelief, relief, thrilled are a few of the adjectives which come to mind.

For the next couple hours I telephoned everyone I could think of for the sole purpose of gloating. Most of my friends were as dumbstruck as I although a few wondered about the wrath that would come upon me when my brother-in-law found out. Frankly, I could have cared less as all I could think of is the Bennett Road property would stay in the family where it belonged.

Later that evening, I called on the woman who was purchasing the property to get the key she had in her possession. She, of course, was very upset as she was buying the home for her daughter. I did feel badly for her and I tried to explain that I was determined to keep the property in the family. I told her if this was not possible, I certainly would contact her immediately.

The next day I telephoned my brother-in-law receiving the ice cold reception I expected. He was angry to say the least. I told him my husband, Bill, (whom he liked) proposed the exact deal he had on the table as we felt sure one of my sons could and would purchase the property, thus keeping it in the family.

Duane had moved to Colorado some twenty years earlier so he still thought of my sons as youngsters. He asked how I thought either of them could afford the property to which I replied the boys had become men and either could purchase it. We hung up.

My son, Roger did in fact buy the property. He then rented the house to the wonderful girl who later became his wife. When later they purchased another fabulous property on the same road, he sold 374 Bennett Road to my nephew, Dan DeRoo, my sister Lonna's son who is slowly remodeling the home and doing a great job.

I am a believer that things work out the way that they are supposed to, even when we are unable to understand. I believe in Angels as well as divine intervention. I believe the Bennett road property was meant to stay in the family and it has.

Just in case any of my readers doubt that is true I must relate one more true story about Bennett road. Shortly after Roger bought the property, Roger and his friend were cleaning out the attic in the greenhouse. Both suited with gloves and facemasks, the two were just pitching items out of the window as fast as they could into a pickup truck below. Before they knew it, the truck was full so they came down the ladder to take the truck load of junk to the dump. To Roger's amazement and surprise sticking out of the top of the load, as though someone had purposely placed it there, Roger saw a wood cross. He leaned down and pulled it out of the pile. A homemade wooden cross. Rog stared at it in wonder as he turned it over. On the back of the cross are the words, Glenn Koss, Hilton, NY.

The cross hangs in Roger's home. Divine intervention? I know what I believe, how about you?

THE CHURCH WINDOW
ST. PAUL LUTHERAN CHURCH

As you enter the sanctuary of St. Paul Lutheran Church on East Avenue in Hilton you pass through double doors. Above the doors is a wonderful round stained glass window which is lighted. The window was in the original St. Paul Lutheran Church when the building was completed at the turn of the century.

My story about the window began years ago in the seventies. But wait a minute, I am ahead of myself. The story really began when I was about to be married. I had been raised in the Greece Baptist Church and wanted to be married there. However, there was a major upheaval in the church at the time and I found that I could not be married by Reverend Dean, a minister of whom I was extremely fond. Glenn suggested that we meet with his minister, Pastor Theodore Kohlmeier, at St. Paul Lutheran Church with the idea that we could be married at St. Paul. The entire Koss family was lifetime members of St. Paul; in fact Glenn's grandfather had been part of the ground breaking ceremony in 1898.

I immediately liked Pastor Kohlmeier, so much so that following our marriage I took adult confirmation classes and became a member of the church. Early in the 1970's, Pastor Kohlmeier retired and his successor was Albert Zoller. Pastor Zoller came with his young family to St. Paul where he was the Pastor for the next thirty plus years.

Often it was obvious, at least to me, how much Pastor Zoller loved the church building as some event of the week past would be reflected in his Sunday sermon. A particular sermon which caught my attention was focused upon Pastor rummaging through the attic of the old church building where he came upon the beautiful stained glass church window. St. Paul had been remodeled in the 1940's; the window removed and relegated to a spot in the attic until such time as the members might find a use for it. Following that sermon I continued to think about the lovely window often wishing I had the funds to do something about a re-installation although I had no idea where that installation would be.

Following Glenn's passing there were some memorial gifts of money. It was my desire to choose something for the church in memory of Glenn. Immediately, the beautiful stained glass window came to mind. Upon investigation there were not the funds available nor was there an idea as to where the window might go in the building. Instead we purchased new acolyte torches. While I was delighted with our memorial, I never forgot about the lovely window with the cross in the middle.

As I write I often mention the passing of time as years seem to fly and again in this instance it is true. Twenty-two years passed when my second husband, Bill Wright died on September 25, 2005 of an aneurysm. Bill was also a member of St. Paul. Bill was an easy going, super guy, well-liked by many in the community as was more than evident by over five hundred people who attended his visitation. Memorial gifts began to pour into the church. Before long we began to realize there was a considerable amount of money so again I began to wonder what happened to the original window. The brand new St. Paul church building had been completed earlier in 2005. When I contacted Pastor Zoller to inquire about the window I was both surprised and delighted to find out the window was in good shape and slated to be a part of the new building. It was to be hung over the double doors with a light installed behind the window. Another amazing fact was that my nephew, Daniel DeRoo, who operated a wood working business, had been commissioned to make a frame for the window as soon as funds were available. Our family was thrilled when we realized there was enough money to cover the cost of the frame which is around the window and the installation of the window.

Thanks to all who contributed a monetary memorial to St. Paul in memory of William E. Wright, the window was hung and dedicated in January, 2006. Currently at the end of each service the Pastor who has walked to the rear of the church announces to the congregation he would like them to focus on the cross in the window above as they receive the Benediction of the Lord.

I look at the window remembering with love two fine men who were a part of my life. While losing each was difficult, I know they are with their Lord this day which is a comfort to those of us who are left.

A special thanks to Dorothy Wright as it was she who contacted me as the memorial fund grew as she was aware that I wanted to choose something for the church that was truly memorable. I want to publically thank each and every contributor. All of you are who made it possible. Thank you.

Years will pass and I too will become a memory. That is the circle of life but the stained glass window in St. Paul sanctuary will be remain for all to see and revere.

A HEAP OF LIVING

(Fiction)

His husky voice broke the silence as he said, "Time to go Mom"

The sound of his voice startled the tiny woman deep in thought as she examined the well-worn brick fireplace. She glanced around at the rest of room now empty as the furniture had either gone in the moving van or been sold at the recent sale. Jeanine continued to sit in silence.

Jeff, her son stood wondering if she had heard him at all. Gently, he touched her shoulder, "Mom, are you ok?" he asked.

A still pretty woman, she gazed at him with a blank stare, her lovely blue eyes misting.

"Just a few more minutes, Honey, then I will be ready to go. Here, take this chair," she said as she slowly rose to her feet. "I am taking it with me."

Jeff, a handsome middle-aged man, looked thoughtfully at his mother as he picked up the chair. Without a word he retreated knowing his mother wanted to be alone.

Jeanine or "Neenie", a fond nickname given her by her husband, scoured each corner of the room as she thought about the first night she entered her brand new house fifty-five years ago. Suddenly she was smiling as she remembered her modern mode of chunky glass lights, aqua, orange and beige the color scheme. They had started a fireplace fire and completed the evening with a champagne toast. She remembered how they laughed because Jim had forgotten to open the fireplace flu. As she recalled that first evening, she found herself caressing the wood of the mantle, her fingers stopping at each little dent in the wood. Those dents were made in less than a minute by a head-strung three year old as he banged on the wood with a rubber hammer, a treasured Christmas gift from his grandmother. Later Neenie would laughingly tell her friends her mantle had been 'antiqued.'

Her eyes darted quickly around the room settling upon the big picture window. Years of the "perfect" Christmas tree flooded her mind. Pondering which tree was the best, she began to wander from empty room to empty room. Looking into each room, Neenie found herself reliving something special about the space. A little room which began as a den, then a nursery and child's room, and now was the upstairs laundry. She glanced at the end of the hall into a room she continued to call Joey's room, her first born. 'Odd, how some things don't change' she mused, 'oh but that thought is wrong, everything changes.'

Continuing the short journey she glanced into her bedroom. She paused at the doorway as she thought of the stories the quiet walls could tell. They would begin with passion and secrets shared, and continue to the laughter, sadness, and even the million tears shed into a pillow. The room had been a "me" place for Jeanine all these years. It was also the spot where her husband had left them forever.

"Mom, it really is time to go." Jeff's voice was growing persistent.

"I know, I am coming," she replied, stopping just long enough to glance in the bathroom mirror as she approved of her new short haircut. 'Funny, she thought, 'I see a happy young woman her whole life in front of her, not the face looking back at me. Surely fifty-five years could not have passed.'

She passed thru the kitchen where imaginary tantalizing smells filled the air. She smelled a turkey or pot roast simmering. She saw a child sitting on the counter licking the frosting bowl. There was merry laughter as friends and family gathered. Carefully Neenie stepped into the family room. As she looked around the large room, she saw a fireplace fire twinkling in the now darkened stone fireplace. She admired the hand hewn beam which had been rescued from an area barn about to be torn down. The window wall of glass facing the west beckoned her for one last look at the wide open field where corn was just sprouting. Her eyes savored the same sight she had enjoyed since the day she married. Her head dropped automatically as she muttered a prayer of thanks that her spot looked exactly the same. Many of her friends had not been as fortunate as their rolling fields had become housing developments, the birds, deer and other wildlife gone.

"Look at those trees, remember when we bought the lot? We walked through brush to tie a sheet around the ones to save and my grandmother's lilac. It is beautiful isn't it?"

Startled, Neenie realized she was talking out loud, her voice echoing in the now empty room. Quickly she tried to gather her composure. 'Stop this,' she admonished herself, 'enough is enough, and you are a survivor!'

Neenie knew her children hated to see her sad so, just as she had done dozens of times, she straightened her shoulders, stuck out her chin, put a smile on her face and determinedly marched to the door.

'Am I like a duck?' she wondered, 'Gliding along so beautifully in the water while their feet are paddling as fast as they can. I just cannot let them know my heart is breaking'

Neenie took one last look at the room in which she had hosted more events that one could remember, Christmas after Christmas, New Year's, St. Patrick's day, showers, weddings, baptisms, and in the last few years far too many funerals. Standing at the door she waved at her son waiting in the car.

"Ok," she hollered perkily, "I am on my way!"

Stepping quickly onto the porch she pulled the door closed behind her. Once in the car, Jeanine fastened her seatbelt as Jeff put the car in gear and began to drive slowly out of the driveway.

"Wait a minute, Jeff, I forgot something."

Automatically Jeff obeyed; however, as he put the car in reverse, he could not help but wonder what his mother would think of next. Jeanine jumped out of the car and was fumbling through a tote on the floorboard where she retrieved a gaily wrapped package. Smiling at him, she dashed up the porch steps with the gait of a young girl opening the door just far enough to deposit the present.

Returning to the car she re-fastened her seatbelt as she stared straight ahead. Usually chatty, she was silent. Her lips were pursed and her face grim. Jeff quickly turned on the radio and for the next few miles they listened to music. Wanting desperately to make this ride easier for this woman he loved, Jeff finally said,

"Mom, do you mind me asking what was in that package?"

Jeanine smiled and seemed relieved that he had broken the silence.

"No, of course not, it is a housewarming present for the Millers. It is a copy of one of my favorite poems, 'It takes a Heap of Living to make a House a Home,' by Edgar A. Guest. I had the poem put into an antique frame."

At that very moment, Jeff made a right hand turn on to a lovely road. Jeanine stopped in mid-sentence to look at the pond which had a fountain cascading water back in to it. It was lovely as several colored lights created a rainbow of colors. Some ducks were floating graciously in the cool waters of the pond causing her to smile broadly given her recent thoughts.

WISTERIA LIVING CENTER was the message the large sign boasted. A senior housing center where a person began by having their own apartment, then as time warranted would move to the next phase of the end of their life. They were at Jeanine's new home.

Jeanine's apartment was on the ground floor of Building 202 and would, of course, be tastefully decorated with her 'most treasured' items. How fortunate she had been that this particular apartment had been recently vacated, the supervisor had announced during their first visit as the living room had sliding glass doors overlooking the woods. Yes, Jeanine had agreed, that was indeed a plus.

Realizing she had been distracted, she turned to Jeff to continue to tell him about her house warming gift.

"You know Jeff, when I was a little girl my Uncle introduced me to poetry by giving me a book which contained the work of several poets. Immediately I fell in love with Edgar Guest because he wrote about daily life. It takes a Heap of Living to make a House a Home is a favorite." Hesitating slightly, her voice dropped as she continued, "Because it does Jeff and I have done it, a heap of living, I mean."

Jeff listened thoughtfully as he glanced at his mother noting how close she was to tears.

"You have done a heap of living Mom, but there is a lot more," he said as he patted her arm.

"I realize that honey, she replied as the car came to a halt, "but here is the problem, I want **those** fifty-five years back."

They sat in silence, neither moving. Suddenly Jeff was terrified. Would this be the end for his mom? Would she give up?

He tried to study her face wishing he could console his mother the same way he had seen her do for others many times in his life. He searched for words, but none came. The silence was deafening when suddenly as quickly as the solemn moment appeared it disappeared as Jeanine took control. With a flair that only she possessed, she tossed back her hair, a smile crossed her face, her sky blue eyes began to twinkle again as she looked at her son and announced,

"Ok, let's go, if there is a new heap waiting I need to get started. I need to make 202A a home!"

Jeff opened the car door, Jeanine hopped out, threw her arms around him, hugging him tightly, as she planted a kiss on his cheek. She took his hand and together they walked toward Wisteria Living Center building 202.

"Do you think they will let me plant flowers?"

Not waiting for an answer, she continued, "And, I know, I will paint the front door, red and put a rocking chair on the porch."

Jeff smiled to himself. Now that is the mom I know. Little did he know Jeanine was thinking there is time for sadness later….. when I am alone; by the way, I *will* make this house a home!

WHERE WERE YOU THE DAY THE WORLD STOPPED TURNING?

Country singer, Alan Jackson, a favorite of mine, wrote a poignant song following the horrific events of September 11, 2001. The title of which is, 'Where were you the day the world stopped turning?' If you have never heard the song, I would like to encourage you to listen. Alan, a writer/composer, captured the feelings of many when he wrote that song.

It occurred to me those of us who are over sixty have experienced many life shattering incidents which when we have cause to re-visit them our minds freeze. We can go back to the day instantly almost as though it were happening again. Many can tell you what the day was like, what time it was when they heard the news, and exactly what they were doing even what clothes they were wearing.

For an example, November 22, 1963, the day that President Kennedy was assassinated I remember well. It was 1:00 pm on a sunny day. I had just put my son down for a nap. As I was expecting my second child I looked forward to a couple of hours of quiet as I watched a favorite soap opera. I was settled on the couch when Walter Cronkite interrupted the program to announce President Kennedy had been shot in Dallas, Texas. I sat there in disbelief when within minutes; he reappeared, tears streaming down his face, and announced the President was dead. Yes, the world stopped turning that day and for several days following as we glued ourselves to televisions as each detail unfolded. We watched the capture of Lee Harvey Oswald. We watched as Jack Ruby shot Oswald in the police station. We watched the funeral procession and saw that adorable little boy salute his father. We watched the riderless horse lead the procession to Arlington Memorial Cemetery. All of America grieved.

Do you recall what you were doing that awful day?

President Kennedy's assassination not only sparked an unsettled time in our history, but many life changing events followed. More leaders gunned down as they went about their lives; Robert Kennedy and Martin Luther King. Our country went through unprecedented racial tension. Do you recall the riots?

The Viet Nam conflict and the Hippie movement were more totally life altering events. Somewhere in there crazy people began to shoot people. Among the first of these tragedies was the Columbine shootings. I was stunned and shocked to believe what I was seeing much less understand what happened. Since that time, it seems that almost daily our hearts break as we hear of unthinkable acts by deranged individuals.

Were you drinking coffee or eating breakfast on the morning of September 11, 2001? Perhaps you were travelling for business or pleasure. It was a Tuesday morning when my friend stopped and told me to turn on TV. We watched in stunned silence and horror. My friend had gone when I heard planes were headed for Washington. I became terrified as my son works for the government. I was babysitting my baby granddaughter and for some unknown reason, I quickly packed her up and took her to the cottage. The cottage is located directly on the shores of Lake Ontario and could have been a bad place to be if we were being invaded. Why did I do that? I do not know. Hours later after I received the call my family was safe, I, like all Americans, sat once again glued to the television. As each unbelievable event unfolded I sat in stunned silence and grief. I continue all these years later to grieve for the victims. I grieve for the children who never knew a parent. I grieve for the heroes who lost their lives somewhere in Pennsylvania. I grieve for every single family affected that terrible day. That evening I took the flag which had covered my husband's casket to my son asking him to raise the flag in honor of all.

During my lifetime, America has survived some seemingly insurmountable events. For the most part America has emerged strong.

History making events will continue to happen. I know the question I am posing will be asked time and time again. However, for today, I ask each of you.

Where were you the day the world stopped turning? What did you do?

THE FUNNIEST THING
HAPPENED......

   Every one of us has experienced some hilarious times in our
lives and since I think we should laugh every day, I decided to
share a few of my favorites.
   When I was twenty-two, Aunt Anna who was in her eighties and
had been very ill died. I had never been part of a funeral before and as
it should be the funeral was a solemn sad event. In those days, it was
common for the family to travel in a limousine to the cemetery. It was
a warm, sunny, summer day. The family was escorted from the
church first, so we were sitting in the limo as the attendees filed out.
The mood was quiet and somber as the church bell pealed.
   I had never been in a limo before so I admit I was quite taken
with the luxury. Electric windows were a novelty as were all the
buttons in the back of the car. The first thing I did was open the
window. At the same minute, Glenn pushed a button which turned
on the radio which unknowingly had the volume turned to high. As
luck would have it the song which was blaring over the church bell
was Louis Armstrong's, "When the Saints go marching in!"
Frantically we pushed buttons finally turning the music off,
however not before a good number of the elder attendees were
entertained. I think Aunt Anna would have laughed although
I must admit we noticed not many others saw the humor.

                          ******

   Our Mom was a good cook whipping up great meals every
day, but she did not like to bake. She really disliked making cakes.
Her sister, Shirley on the other hand, loved baking creating
everything she ever made totally from scratch. One day Aunt Shirl
stopped to see Mom who was attempting to frost a rather lop sided

layer cake. She was sputtering and muttering that she hated baking so Aunt Shirley, trying to be helpful said,

"Berenice if you don't like to bake, why don't you try one of those new mixes that is in the grocery store?"

Mom tossed her spatula in the sink as she exclaimed, "That IS *a mix!*"

******

My sister Lonna was expecting her third child any day when she took her small daughter to pick out new eye glasses at Waldert's Optical Store which was located at Northgate Plaza, in Greece, NY. Upon her return home she immediately called me exclaiming I was not going to believe what happened to her that day.

Lonna related she had several appointments that day. When she arrived to order the glasses, the young man asked for the glasses prescription. He disappeared, only to immediately re-appear, suppressing obvious laughter. He handed the paper back to her muttering something about a mistake. My sister turned scarlet as she looked at the paper she had given him and realized she mistakenly had pulled the wrong prescription from her purse. The prescription she gave him was for birth control pills. Lonna never went to Waldert's again!

******

How about the lady who contacted the highway department to ask if they would change the deer crossing signs on her road to a different spot so that the deer would be crossing in a safer place?

******

Do you recall the large video cameras which were so popular when video cameras first came out? The camera looked like you were taping a breaking news story as you marched around with them on your shoulder. Bill and I bought the latest and greatest RCA color camera. That particular year we went to the Thousand Islands with a group of friends.

The men went fishing. Bill, my husband, caught a trophy fish. All of the men were examining the fish when a friend grabbed the camera to capture the moment. As one watches the video, you see the fish, followed by our friend asking Bill how to turn the camera on. The camera was on, so next you see all the men staring at the camera as Bill announces that the camera is running. With this news Harry, the cameraman, scans the rocky shore to take a picture of the fish which is nowhere to be found. While the men were discussing the camera operation the fish seized the moment to swim to freedom. Next scene the camera pans the faces of the fishermen. The look on each of their faces priceless!

******

Out of the mouths of Babes

Over the years, an expression which I have been known to utter often is 'Damn it.' Not that I am really proud of blurting out the words, however, I have been known to express it loudly repeating the phrase several times. My granddaughter Lauren, 5 at the time, had visited us. Upon her return home, she pulled opened the pantry door causing several cans of soup to fall onto the floor. She put her hands on her hips and uttered, "Damn it, Damn it, Damn it!

Her mother immediately reprimanded her and asked her where she had heard those words. Lauren would not tell her. Finally in exasperation, her mother asked her if she heard it from her Nonnie (me) and defiantly she said,

"No I did not! I heard it from Grandpa and Uncle Roger, not Nonnie!"

******

I could not decide which incident to share about my granddaughter Paige so will let you choose which is the most humorous.

When Paige was three years old her mother and I took her to see some fireworks. She asked if she could have some popcorn.

Her mother said yes, got out of the car, and turned to lift her out. As she jumped in her mother's arms, Paige hollered,

"Hey Momma grab some bucks out of Nonnie's purse and let's go!"

******

A few years ago from an infomercial I bought a Magic Bullet food processor for my kitchen. It was one of those deals that if you make the telephone call immediately you received two units rather than one. I decided to give one to Paige's parents. Paige was helping her mother get the box out of the car and her mother told her to be careful because the Magic Bullet had cost Nonnie a lot of money. Paige promptly replied, "No it didn't Momma, it was a buy one get one free!"

******

My all-time favorite Paige story was when Paige was in Nursery school two days a week. Once in a while it was a struggle to keep her moving along so we would not be late for school. Such was the case one very snowy winter day. As I tried to hurry her along, she became really annoyed with me and me with her. Finally we got into the car and I drove to the school. As I drove along, I glanced into the rear view mirror to see a little girl, with huge brown eyes, her head covered with a fuzzy purple hat my sister had made for her, seeming to be deep in thought. She looked so angelic the incident just a few minutes before was forgotten. Out of the blue she suddenly asked,

"Nonnie, is it a bad thing to stick up your third finger when you are mad?" Not sure how I should reply, I finally answered, "Well Paige that is not something a young lady would do."

A couple minutes passed when quietly I heard, "Sorry Nonnie, cause that is what I did to you when you made me mad!"

I almost drove directly into a snow bank!

YOU ARE THE AUTHOR OF YOUR OWN STORY!

Fall is my favorite season of the year. The crisp cool days along with the fabulous colors seem to soothe my soul. Often when enjoying the beauty of the season I find myself gazing at the foliage as if it were the first time I have ever seen the brilliance. As I have been working upon finishing this book during the fall of 2012, the season has to me been exceptional in color as everywhere I look I see wonderful shades of yellow, green, red, orange, gold blending together as if someone had carefully selected each tree and placed it next to the tree which will compliment it the most. Yes, it is my opinion fall in the Northeast is glorious.

During this time of year, I often think of my Aunt Kathryn Cole Irons. Aunt Kay, my mother's sister, was an artist who taught Art at Greece Central School. She was a talented beautiful woman who died far too young in 1983. One day during a visit we were discussing the seasons when Kay mentioned that fall was her favorite as well, exclaiming that when she got to Heaven she intended to pick up her palette and paint the beautiful colors. On a particularly lovely day I like to think she is painting the scene at which I am gazing.

Kay was a woman far ahead of her time and a woman of great faith. She did not see fall as the end of the year she saw it as a new beginning. I feel the same way. I see it as a wonderful season which will be followed by another wonderful season. It is during those seasons that life experiences happen. Each and every one of us has fascinating incidents to relate whether in a book that is published or writing for your family. Aunt Kay was an artist so she left a legacy in her art but her stories are gone.

My mother's other sister, Shirley Cole Murphy, has also passed as have the many hilarious incidents of her life. During the last few years of her life I tried to convince her to let me interview her so I could capture memories for her family.

Aunt Shirl had lived through the depression. She had vivid memories of World War II and she possessed a marvelous sense of humor. Just as we remember no television, no microwave, computers, cell phones, certainly no self-cleaning ovens or refrigerators with a water dispenser, she remembered the ice box, early cars, picking cherries and life on the farm...stories that I wish we could have preserved.

I do understand the hesitancy as we think nothing particularly unusual or earth shaking has occurred in our lives. However, something significant has happened in every life and it should be captured. My own mother, Berenice Cole Lowden felt the same as her sisters. Little did she know how precious a letter or note in her handwriting would become once she was gone.

So my message is the message portrayed on a plaque given me by a friend... **You are the Author of your own Life Story**!

Please, grab a pad and jot down your memories. When your kids or grandkids say something which strikes your heart, write it down. If you are hesitant to write or do not think you are able try making a tape and if that will not work find someone to write for you. Call me, I will help you.

Trust me - someday your family will truly thank you.

RANDOM THOUGHTS FOR FAMILY & FRIENDS

As a final chapter to my book and so that perhaps many years from now someone will read my offerings and try to imagine what kind of a person I was while here on earth, it came to me that I would attempt to write a few of my thoughts on life.

Many years ago there was a dance at the Greece Town Hall. My mother made me an outfit, the skirt was made of brown velvet. At the bottom of the skirt there was a spot in the velvet. My mom being very creative pulled up the skirt and attached a bow so that the full petticoat showed just a touch. I loved the outfit, my friends did not. They made fun of my skirt and I began to cry. Dad overheard them and took me aside. He told me how pretty I looked and how my friends did not mean what they said. He then taught me one of the most important lessons of my life. He said to never be a follower, to play music to my own drum, be strong, take people for what they are and to try to find something good in everyone. The advice he offered to that heartbroken little girl helped mold me into the adult I became. It is my hope I have passed this philosophy on to my family since it is my belief that if one can follow his advice, no matter the obstacles, one can succeed in having a happy life full of love, friends and family. I know that I have been truly blessed with a wonderful family, lots of love, and many friends each of whom I consider special. I treasure their friendships and miss them daily when I can no longer see them.

As our ever changing world evolves I feel strongly that I do not and will not change my belief just to be up-to-date. For example, I think casual sex is wrong. I believe the marvelous intimate relationship should be special. I believe that, while I judge no one as to their preference, the institution of marriage should be between a man and a woman. I believe our society would not have nearly the turmoil were married couples to try a bit harder to stay together until their family is grown. I believe parenting is the most difficult job in the world. I believe it is alright to say no.

I believe people should stand, remove their hats and cross their heart when our National Anthem is played. I believe people should practice their religion. There will come a time when every single person will find comfort in being able to cling to a power far greater than them.

I believe in saying Merry Christmas. I believe laughter is the best medicine. I believe in smiling at people I do not know. I believe I am so happy I was given a sense of humor so that I can tell all who are reading this that I believe you just might be tired of reading what I believe so I believe I will write these two words....

THE END